GROSS MOTOR ACTIVITIES
FOR YOUNG CHILDREN WITH
SPECIAL NEEDS

By
Carol Huettig, Ph.D
Jean Pyfer, P.E.D
David Auxter, Ed.D

A supplement to:
Auxter • Pyfer • Huettig
Principles and Methods of
Adapted Physical Education and Recreation

Tenth Edition

Boston   Burr Ridge, IL   Dubuque, IA   Madison, WI   New York   San Francisco   St. Louis
Bangkok   Bogotá   Caracas   Lisbon   London   Madrid   Mexico City
Milan   Montreal   New Delhi   Santiago   Seoul   Singapore   Sydney   Taipei   Toronto

The **McGraw·Hill** Companies

McGraw-Hill Higher Education

Gross Motor Activities for Young Children with Special Needs to accompany
PRINCIPLES AND METHODS OF ADAPTED PHYSICAL EDUCATION
AND RECREATION, Tenth Edition
Carol Huettig, Jean Pyfer, and David Auxter

Published by McGraw-Hill Higher Education, an imprint of The McGraw-Hill
Companies, Inc.,
1221 Avenue of the Americas, New York, NY 10020. Copyright © 2005, 2001,
1993 by The McGraw-Hill Companies, Inc. All rights reserved.

This book is printed on acid-free paper.

1 2 3 4 5 6 7 8 9 0 BKM/BKM   0 9 8 7 6 5 4

ISBN 0-07-294452-8

www.mhhe.com

PREFACE

This handbook of more than 200 activities and suggested songs has been developed as a resource for physical educators, adapted physical educators and early childhood educators serving young children. Children of all ability levels will enjoy these child-tested activities, but most importantly, children with developmental delays and disabilities will derive significant benefit. Each activity has been carefully selected to promote central nervous system development.

Equilibrium
The development of equilibrium is critical in the development of motor function. Equilibrium is essential in maintaining one's balance while rolling, crawling, creeping, walking, running or when performing any other motor activity. The activities included in this section have been selected to ensure that children develop these critical postural reactions while having fun.

Sensory Stimulation and Discrimination
For children to learn to discriminate among different types of touch, body movements, sounds, and sights, it is necessary for them to experience a variety of these sensations. Activities in this section are designed to stimulate the tactile, vestibular, proprioceptive, auditory, and visual systems.

Body Image
A well-developed body image helps children to understand their movement capabilities. The activities in this section help children identify their individual body parts, develop a whole body concept, and practice using their body in a variety of ways.

Basic Locomotor Skills

Mastery of basic locomotor patterns is required before a child can participate successfully in play, games, leisure, recreation and sport activities and are critical to activities of daily living, as well. The activities in this section provide children the opportunity to practice modifying the variables of time, space, force and flow of their movements.

Motor Planning

The motor planning activities in this section help children learn to anticipate, predict, and plan their movements.

Object Control Skills

The ability to receive and propel objects in the environment is critical for many play, games, leisure, recreation and sport activities. The activities in this section give children the chance to develop basic eye-hand, eye-foot, and eye-body control skills.

Cross-Lateral Integration

Cross-lateral integration is the ability to coordinate the two sides of the body during movement. Until this integration develops, children tend to use each side of the body independently and have problems with any activities requiring the use of their limbs at or across the midline (center) of the body. The activities in this section require the child to continually move beyond the midline.

Aerobic Fitness

Cardiovascular endurance is a critical component of wellness and health. The activities, particularly useful for in-seat and "circle-time" activities, focus on aerobic activities that will enhance cardiovascular endurance.

Animal Actions

Young children like to "pretend to be" animals. These animal actions help children develop equilibrium, sensory discrimination, body image, motor planning, locomotor competency and strength/fitness. The activities are included throughout the book.

Cooperative Play and Games

Cooperative games are included to enable young children with a variety of abilities to work together. Parallel and cooperative play are developmentally appropriate for young children.

The delightful clip art is from www.arttoday.com.

We hope this handbook will prove to be a useful tool. We encourage you to contact us or our publisher, Mc-Graw Hill, with any comments or suggestions for improvement.

Carol Huettig, Ph.D
Jean Pyfer, PED
David Auxter, Ed.D

TABLE OF CONTENTS

GROSS MOTOR ACTIVITIES

FOR YOUNG CHILDREN WITH

SPECIAL NEEDS

SUPINE EQUILIBRIUM
Struggling Turtle
Ask the child to lie on her back and pretend to struggle to roll over, by alternating flexing/extending arms and legs. Throughout, the head should be tucked to the chest. When the turtle "struggles" hard enough, the teacher can help roll the turtle over onto her stomach. Before doing the activity, read a story about a turtle or, better still, let them watch a turtle stuck on his back.

Protect the Treasure
Place a bean bag or koosch ball on the child's tummy. Ask the child to lie on his back until the "robber" tries to steal the treasure. To keep from losing the treasure, the child should "tuck" according to ability. For example, one child may just tuck his chin to protect the treasure, while another may have to tuck into a ball to protect the treasure.

Balloon Bobble/Group Bobble
While lying on her back, with head tucked to chest, ask the child to keep a balloon (or a bunch of balloons tied together) up in the air, using hands, feet, elbows, and knees. If the child is unable to perform the activity alone, the teacher may have to help by bouncing the balloon off the child's body. Several children can do this together with their feet in the center of a circle.

Supine Scooter Play
Involve the child in any type of supine scooter activity with the chin tucked. Use large scooters for children with poor equilibrium and poor muscle tone.

Puppy on a Leash
Ask the child to lie on his back on a scooterboard holding one end of a rope. A teacher or another child can pull the "puppy" around the room.

Crossing the Alligator Pit

Suspend a rope over the child at arms length from her chest. Ask the child, lying supine on a scooterboard, to pull herself, hand over hand, the length of the rope, headfirst.

Recliner Cycling

Ask the child to lie on his back and pedal his legs like he is riding a bicycle [chin tucked]. This can be done with partners as well. Ask two children to lie down with the balls of their feet together and bicycle.

Rock 'n Roll

When working with a child with profound disabilities, lie down and hold the child on your chest, with his back on your stomach. Hold the child tightly and roll, gently, from side to side.

PRONE EQUILIBRIUM
Superchild

Ask the child to lie on her tummy on a scooterboard and, holding arms and head up in the air [like Superman flying] "fly" after a teacher's push.

Peeking Turtle

The child lies on his tummy, chin tucked to his chest, with his head covered by a small bean bag chair. The turtle "peeks" out by lifting his head.

Hungry Alligators

Ask the children to crawl on their stomachs. Ask one child to be the "hungry" alligator. On cue, the "hungry" alligator tries to bite the others [using hands/arms extended and clapping to simulate biting action]. Each "bitten" alligator then becomes a "hungry" alligator until all are bitten. [This is great on scooters, too.]

Tummy Ball Balance

Ask a child to lie on her tummy over the top of a large ball with hands and feet touching the floor. Ask the child to try to lift her hands and, then, feet off the floor.

Sneaky Snake

Ask the children to lie on the floor [on tummy on floor or scooterboard]. Call a child's name and repeat the chant:" Here comes a snake, crawling right to me, A long, thin wiggly [child's name] snake I see."

Bean Bag Chair "Swimmer"

Ask the child to lie on his tummy on top of a bean bag chair. Encourage the child to swim using his arms and legs.

Swimmer

Ask the child to lie in the center of a parachute held by friends and teachers. The child pretends to swim on "little ripples" and then "big waves."

Clapping Seal

The child pulls her lower body along the floor, while supporting her body in a push-up position. The child stops, occasionally to rock and "clap fins" and make a seal "honk." If the child is unable to support self in this position, the child's chest could be supported by a bolster or pillow.

4

Wheelbarrow   Walk
Supporting part of the child's body weight on a bolster, rolled-up mat, or pillow, ask the child to walk on his hands while the teacher holds the child just above the knees. [Child can walk on his forearms.]

SITTING   EQUILIBRIUM
Sitting   "Tug-of-War"
Ask two children to sit on the floor, facing each other, and play "tug-of-war" with a ball, rope, or soft toy.
Modify the activity by asking the children to sit on a rolled mat or on pillows while playing "tug."

Tandem Seat Walk
Have two children sit in a straddle position, one behind the other; the child in back cradles the child in front. Ask them to shift their weight together to "shuffle" while sitting.   The teacher can seat a child on her legs to teach the "shuffle."

Row, Row, Row Your Boat
Ask two children to sit, facing each other, with crossed legs. Holding hands, sing the song with the following modifications:
• Row, row, row your boat [moving front and back],
• Tilt, tilt, tilt your boat [moving front and back while tilting left and right],
• Rock, rock, rock your boat [rock all over].

Sitting   Bounce
Ask a child to sit on a large therapy or playground ball, while holding her teacher's hands. The teacher should move the hands to force the child into "disequilibrium." Then the child must regain an upright, sitting position.

Humpty Dumpty

Ask the children to sit and tuck into a tight ball, while they chant: "Humpty Dumpty sat on a wall...Humpty Dumpty had a great fall...[the children tumble over]...All the queen's horses and all the queen's men...Couldn't put Humpty together again." [The children try to roll -- egg-like -- to regain a sitting position].

HANDS AND KNEES EQUILIBRIUM

Robin Hood

Ask two children to assume all-fours positions on hands and knees next to each other, each facing the opposite direction. Shifting weight, each child should attempt to push the other child off balance.

Ball Straddle

Ask a child to lie over the top of a big playground ball or therapy ball, keeping hands and knees in contact with the ground. Ask the child to lift hands and knees, individually at first, and then all four, off the ground.

Puppy with a Sore Paw

The child starts on hands and knees and then moves on only three of the body parts, while whimpering.

Cow Eating Her Cud

Ask the child to move on all fours, while pushing a bean bag or koosch ball with his nose. The child should stop every so often to "chew his cud."

Bunny Hop

The child assumes a hands and knees position [with lower leg in contact with the floor]. The child moves both hands forward together and then pulls (slides) both legs up towards the hands [a homologous movement].

Buckin' Bronco

Ask the child to assume an all-fours position. Put a small bean bag chair, pillow, or large bean bags on the child's back and ask the child to "buck" to get the "cowgirl" off her back.

Dizzy Dog

The child creeps on hands and knees, but crosses her right arm in front of the left one, in an "X." Change the lead arm.

Dinosaur Walk

The child moves on all-fours, homolaterally [right hand and right knee, then left hand and left knee], while the children chant "Di-No-Saur," "Di-No-Saur."

Angry Kitty

The child assumes an all-fours position on the floor. Hissing loudly, the "kitty" presses his back up to form an arch. Ask the child to hold the position while "hissing" and then to relax. This can be turned into a delightful game by letting one child be a "puppy"...enjoy the "hissing" and "barking."

The Bear Went Over the Mountain

The child moves on all fours using hands and feet. The bear lumbers [right hand and right foot move together, left hand and left foot move together] while singing the "Bear Went Over the Mountain."

Froggy

The child assumes a semi-squat position and springs forward to another semi-squat position. Do not allow the child to move into full flexion at the knee. This is much more fun if the child springs from lily pad [carpet square or poly-spot] to lily pad while shouting "ribbid."

Mad Mule

The child places his hands on the floor and gently kicks his legs up into the air, supporting his body weight on his hands. If the child is unable to support his body weight, modify the activity by having the child lie over the top of a bolster or large therapy ball.

KNEELING EQUILIBRIUM
Mirror

Ask two children to face each other while kneeling. Have one child move while the other "mirrors" the action. [It may be necessary to let the children practice moving while looking into a real mirror.]

Palm Pressure

Kneeling, ask two children to play "mirror" but this time their palms should be touching. They try to push each other over.

Pillow Fight
Ask two children to kneel and, using pillows, try to push each other off balance.

STANDING EQUILIBRIUM
Balance Board
Ask the child to stand on a balance board and try to keep both edges of the board from touching the floor.

Ostrich
Ask the child to stand on one foot and recite: "Silly bird, silly bird...one foot down. Silly bird, silly bird...Don't fall down."

GENERAL EQUILIBRIUM ACTIVITIES
Magic Carpet Ride
Ask the child to assume one of the following positions: supine, prone, sitting, or kneeling on a mat, blanket, or quilt. Grasp the edge of the mat and pull the child about as if on a magic carpet. Several children can sit on the mat and several can help pull.

Crazy Sidewalk
Place soft objects [bean bag chairs, pillows, rolled up towels] under a quilt or blanket so the surface of the mat is lumpy, uneven, and variable. Ask the child to perform a locomotor skill with which the child is comfortable: crawl, creep, hands and knees walk, knee walk, walk, run, jump and, for variety, do each of these backwards.

Parachute Rock n' Roll

Ask the children and adults to sit around a parachute or a colored sheet. The children on the outside grasp the parachute, lean back and make "little ripples" or "big waves." Ask a child to roll, crawl, creep, hands and knees walk, etc._ across the parachute.

SENSORY STIMULATION   AND DISCRIMINATION
TACTILE ACTIVITIES

Partner Massage

Teach children to give each other a massage. Introduce deep pressure along the long bones of the body [spine and long bones in the legs and arms]. When applying deep pressure, the child should use the fleshy part of the thumbs to stroke the length of the bone.

Texture Rub

Rub the child with materials that have different textures [silk, feathers, sponges, brushes, fake animal fur, flannel]. At first, introduce something very rough and then something very smooth.

Taco

Ask several children to lie on one-half of a parachute and pretend to be meat, cheese, or beans for the taco. Ask other children to add the filling [jalapeno peppers, tomatoes, cheese, etc...using bean bags, koosch balls]. Then pull the empty half of the parachute over the top of all the children.

Hot Dog

Stuff a child between two bean bag chairs. Add condiments. Let other children start to nibble from each end.

Hamburger

Ask the child to lie on a bean bag chair on her back or tummy. Add the stuff the child wants on the hamburger [chocolate sprinkles...yes a real child's request..., ketchup, or pickles using bean bags, koosch balls, etc.] Then put another bean bag chair on top of the child.

Build a Fire

Ask two children to lie face down on a mat or quilt. Help another child lie on top of the other two, placed as if stacking logs. As the children get more comfortable, increase the base to three, then four children.

Water Play [Sponge It...]

Let the children throw water-soaked sponge squares. Cut the sponges into 2" squares. [A whole sponge gets too heavy]. This is particularly fun in the sun or in the pool.

Water Play [Sprinkle or Hose It]

Allow the children to move in any way under a sprinkler or through water coming out of a hose.

Water Play [Slip, Sliding Away]

Build your own "slip and slide" with plastic garbage bags [available commercially, but expensive]. Let the children crawl, creep, or knee-walk on the plastic. It's very slippery...so don't let the children stand or walk.

Body Painting

Ask one child to paint a partner's body part with shaving cream, whipped cream, or pudding. For example, "Ernesto, paint Theresa's foot with pudding."

11

Texture Play
Allow the child to play in a large box or child's wading pool filled with sand, styrofoam peanuts, popcorn, oatmeal, uncooked beans, uncooked rice, puffed rice, or small plastic balls. [McDonalds and other companies with "playlands" will donate their used balls.]

Mummy Maker
Ask a partner to wrap another child with toilet paper or paper towels. [Good for little ones]. The idea is to have the "mummy" wrapped so that only the child's eyes are peeking out. Taking a picture of the mummy is cool.

Shape Maker
Draw a simple shape on the child's back, forehead, arms, legs or palms. Ask the child to identify the shape without "peeking." Note: If the child peeks, the child needs to peek.

VESTIBULAR   ACTIVITIES
Vestibular stimulation has to be carefully monitored. Cease any activity if the child becomes flushed, pale, or nauseous.

Rock n'Roll
Ask the child to roll one turn to the right, one to the left, two to the right, two to the left, etc.

Scooter-Spin
Ask the child to lie prone or sit on a scooter and spin self. If the child asks to spin faster, the teacher can help.

Helicopter
Grab the child's hands and begin to turn in a circle. As you move faster, the child's feet should get further off the floor.

Swinging on Swings
If the child is unable to swing on the swing set independently, let the child sit on your lap while you swing.

PROPRIOCEPTIVE   ACTIVITIES
Songs and Dances
Ask the children to bend, stretch, twist, or curl specific body parts. The following songs, on the Walter the Waltzing Worm tape by Hap Palmer are particularly good: What a Miracle
Walter the Waltzing Worm
Flick a Fly

Push, Pull and Carry
Ask the child to push, pull and carry a variety of objects of different size, shape, weight, and sizes. For example, ask the child to walk on a 4" balance beam while carrying a tennis ball in one hand and a 2# hand weight in the other.

Thumb, Arm, and Leg Wrestle
Encourage two children to thumb, arm or leg wrestle.

Simon Says
Play "Simon Says" focusing on a variety of body parts.

Stationary Statue Maker
Have the teacher or another child be the "statue maker." The statue maker should carefully place the "statue's body" in a particular position. The statue can be as complex or as simple as needed for each child. Ask the child to hold the statue position.

Gumby Lives
Put a gumby or a rag doll into a given position on the floor. Ask the child to assume the same position.

Jump Rope Pattern
Place a jump rope on the floor. Ask the child to lie down, following the path of the rope.

Stick Figures
Draw a stick figure on the blackboard or draw a figure on butcher paper or the sidewalk and ask the children to replicate the position.

Angels in the Snow
Ask the child to lie down on her back on brown butcher paper. Holding crayons in both hands, ask the child to move her arms, maintaining contact with the paper throughout.

AUDITORY ACTIVITIES
Move to the Music
Ask the children to take turns "making music" with pots and pans or musical instruments. Ask the other children to crawl, creep, walk, run, etc. to the beat of the music.

14

Follow My Moves
Ask a child to beat a drum, following the "rolling" or "walking" of another child. The moving child can speed up or slow down and then the drummer speeds up or slows down in response. This is a particularly great activity for a child with limited volitional movement; she can beat the drum while playing with another child.

Animal Sounds
Have the children listen to a tape or song with animal sounds. Ask the children to duplicate the sounds while pretending to be the animal.

Special Sound
Ask the children to listen to a new song and clap, stomp, jump or raise their hands when they hear a particular word.

Follow the Teacher's Sound
Ask the children to use any locomotor activity to follow the teacher's singing or humming around the room with their eyes closed. Note: if the child peeks, he needs to peek.

Beep Ball Roll
Ask two children to sit, each facing a partner. With eyes closed, the children roll a beep ball back and forth between their legs. Start with the children's feet touching so their legs form a diamond.

Hide a Beep Ball
Hide a beeping ball and ask the children to try to find the ball with eyes closed. Note: if the child peeks, she needs to peek.

15

Follow My Music
Give each child a musical instrument [homemade or "store-bought"]. Ask one child to create a beat/pattern and then ask the others to follow the beat/pattern with their movements.

Follow the Bouncing Ball
Ask a child to throw a ball high into the air. The other children shake, beat, or strike their instrument each time the ball bounces.

Watch the Balloon
Ask the children to track the flight of a balloon with their eyes. Ask the children to point at the balloon with their index fingers. Tie several balloons together.

Follow the Scarves
Ask the children to track the flight of a scarf the teacher drops above the child's head. As the child develops the skills to track and catch one, add another scarf.

Bubble Blowing
Blow bubbles and ask the child to break the bubble with a pointed finger.

Follow the Flashlight
Darken the room. Ask a child to follow the circle of light created with a flashlight. The child can crawl, creep, walk, run, jump or hop to follow the circle of light.

Picture Taker

Ask a child to move about the room and pretend to take pictures with a camera. When she has finished taking the pictures, ask the child to describe the pictures she took. Start simply with one or two pictures. Then build to more.

BODY IMAGE
Sock Walk

Have the child put her hands into clean socks. Draw shoes or boots with magic markers on the socks. Then let the child "walk" or "run" or "tiptoe" or "dance" on the body part named. For example, "Lisa, tiptoe on your tummy."

Gumby or Raggedy Ann

Place a Gumby doll in a specific body position. Ask the child to duplicate Gumby's position. You can do the same thing with a Raggedy Ann or Raggedy Andy doll.

Angel Making

Ask the child to make an "angel," lying flat on his back, and then flat on his stomach. First have the child move homologously [arms and legs move together]. Second, have the child move homolaterally [arms and legs on one side of the body move together]. Third, have the child move contralaterally [left arm moves with right leg and right arm moves with left leg]. Do this in a clean sandbox or on a surface that has been dusted with chalk.

Tunnels

Ask several children to get on hands and feet and make a tunnel for other children to crawl through. Make the tunnels more elaborate by adding chairs or tables with sheets or blankets draped over them.

17

Other Objects and Me
Give the child every opportunity to relate her known body parts to other objects. For example, "Can you lie on your tummy on the floor?" "Can you put a knee or elbow on the bean bag?" "Can you put your gluteous maximus in the hula hoop?"

Move in Patterns
Ask the child if he can move himself in a particular pattern. "Can you crawl on this Figure 8?" "Can you walk on this triangle?" "Can you walk backwards on the outline of the stop sign?"

3-D and Me
Give the child every possible opportunity to explore the relationship between her body and large, open 3-dimensional objects. "Can you climb into that box?" "Can you and a friend fit into the box together?"

Simon Says
The teacher or another student should assume the role of "Simon." Ask the child to do activities, at their own level, which require them to identify their body parts. "Simon says, touch your nose." "Simon says, touch your right ear with your left hand."

Shadow Maker
Ask the children to take turns making "shadows" in front of the overhead projector screen. It is particularly fun if you put butcher paper on the screen and trace the "shadow."

Rubber Band Magic
Using a huge rubber band or large strip of cloth, ask several children to make shapes using the rubber band and their bodies.

Play Horsey
Ask the children to move while holding another object, or prop, like playing "horsey."

Twister
Play the commercial game "Twister" or make your own "Twister" game on a felt-backed vinyl tablecloth, or draw with chalk on a sidewalk. The child is asked to put a hand on a red dot, a foot on a blue square, etc. You can make this as simple or complex as its needs to be to meet the children's needs. This can be used to teach other concepts, as well.

My Own Hands or Feet
Make tracings of each child's hands and feet. Then let the children color their hands and feet.

Move in a Smaller Space
Let the children explore their bodies in slowly decreasing space. For example, ask the children to walk or roll their wheelchairs backward without touching anyone or anything. Slowly decrease the amount of space in which they can move.

My Own Body Puzzle
Make "butcher paper" tracings of each child's body. Then make "My Own Body" puzzles for each child by laminating and then cutting up the traced body. Initially, the child can have a puzzle that is only the top half and lower half of the body. Then, the puzzle can get more sophisticated, including arms and legs, and head.

Make a Shape
Ask a small group of children to create shapes with their bodies.
- "Can you and three friends make a triangle with your bodies?
- "Can you and a partner make a rectangle?
- "Can you and your friends make a cube?

Sugar Shadow
Make "powdered sugar" tracings of the child. Ask the child to lie on the floor and shake powdered sugar from a small canister around the child's frame. Then, help the child get up without disturbing the shadow.

Footprints in the Sand
Ask the child to walk through the sandbox and look at her footprints. Then ask the child to walk through the sandbox again, placing her feet in the same spots. Ask another child to walk through the sandbox, placing his feet in the footprints that already exist.

Footprints

Ask the child to put her feet in tempera paint and then walk on a large piece of paper. Be sure to hold the child's hand as the paint can be slippery. This activity also works if the child simply puts feet in the water in a bucket and then walks on concrete.

Rhythmic Activities

The following songs/dances are really effective in developing body image in little ones:

Walter the Waltzing Worm, Hap Palmer

What a Miracle
Walter the Waltzing Worm
Flick a Fly
Swing, Shake, Twist and Bend

Sally the Swinging Snake, Hap Palmer

Sally the Swinging Snake
On the Count of Five

Preschool Favorites, Georgiana Stewart

Warm-Up Time
Bendable Stretchable
Bean Bag Rock

Six Little Ducks, Kimbo

The Wheels on the Bus

LOCOMOTOR PATTERNS

The goal of gross motor programming is for the child to "own" a variety of locomotor skills. "Ownership" means that the child can perform a locomotor skill automatically and without conscious thought. In order to own a specific locomotor skill, the child must have the opportunity to use the skill in a variety of situations and circumstances. This can be done by manipulating and using the four primary variables of movement:

- Time
- Space
- Force
- Flow

Locomotor Skill: Roll

Modifying the variable of TIME, ask the child to:
Roll fast.
Roll slow.
Roll, gradually increasing speed.
Roll down an incline, gradually increasing speed.
Roll, gradually decreasing speed.
Go on a "Rolling Ride."

> Ask the child to lie down on the edge of a sheet or blanket on a carpet or mat. Roll the child gently in the sheet or blanket. When the child is wrapped up, grab the edge of the sheet and lift it so the child rolls out quickly.

Modifying the variable of SPACE, ask the child to:
Roll with arms at the sides of the body.
Roll with arms above the head.

Roll with a partner.

> Partners should face each other and wrap arms around each other. Holding on tightly, they should roll together.

Modifying the variable of FORCE, ask the child to:

Roll hard.

Roll gently.

Roll in a carpeted barrel.

Do a "Rocking roller."

> Ask the child to lie in the middle of a sheet or blanket. The teacher and other children should hold the edges of two ends of the sheet. Alternately, lift the sheet edges so the child rolls toward one end of the sheet, and then rolls back to the other end of the sheet.

Modifying the variable of FLOW, ask the child to:

Roll in one direction; stop; roll in the other direction.

Roll; stop; roll; stop; roll; and stop.

Play "I Can Escape."

> Roll the child into a sheet or blanket. Tell the child to try to get out as quickly as possible. At first, you may need to leave an arm and leg unwrapped.

Do different types of rolls:

- Log roll [whole body moves as a unit.]
- Segmental roll [head leads shoulder, leads hips.]
- Egg roll [child tucks and holds ankles with hands.]
- Shoulder roll.
- Forward roll.
- Backward roll.

Locomotor Skill: Crawl

Modifying the variable of TIME, ask the child to:
Crawl fast, crawl faster, crawl faster yet.
Crawl and stop. Crawl and stop.
> Use "The Freeze."

Modifying the variable of SPACE, ask the child to:
Crawl to a favorite doll or toy.
Crawl through a tunnel made of chairs or sheets.
Crawl through an obstacle course made of pillows,
> rolled towels, and bean bag chairs going over,
> under, around and through the objects.

Crawl under classmates' spread legs.
Crawl backwards.
Crawl backwards on a circle on the floor.

Modifying the variable of FORCE, ask the child to:
Crawl pushing a ball with her nose.
Crawl with a partner riding on his back.
Crawl with small weights [less than 1 pound]
> attached to her wrists and ankles.

Modifying the variable of FLOW, ask the child to:
Crawl up an incline; stop; turn around; crawl down.
Crawl in a circle; stop; crawl backwards on the
> same circle.

Locomotor Skill: Creep

Modifying the variable of TIME, ask the child to:
Creep to fast music. Creep to slow music.
Creep to a drum beat that gets ever slower, until
> The child is moving as if in slow motion.

Modifying the variable of SPACE, ask the child to:
Creep forward, with a bean bag on the child's head.
Creep over classmates lying face down in a row,
        with spaces between them.
Creep under a series of desks or tables.

Modifying the variable of FORCE, ask the child to:
Creep through sand, water [small wading pool], tall
        grass, etc.
Creep while pushing a classmate on a scooter.

Modifying the variable of FLOW, ask the child to:
Creep forward 10 feet; stop; creep backward 10
        feet.
Creep; pause; creep; pause; creep; pause.
Creep; rock on all fours; creep.

Locomotor Skills: Walk/Run

Modifying the variable of TIME, ask the child to:
March to one of the following songs:
Consider Yourself   Preschool Aerobic Fun
Marching Along   Preschool Aerobic Fun

Ask the child to do a "happy walk."
Ask the child to do a "sad walk."
Walk/run to the beat of a drum or the shake of a
        tambourine.

Modifying the variable of SPACE, ask the child to:

Walk/run keeping feet on a line at least as wide as the child's shoulders. As the child becomes more proficient, gradually narrow the width of the line.

Walk/run on a pattern on the floor -- square, circle, triangle, stop sign, number or letter.

Walk/run on a complex pattern -- Figure 8 or zig-zag.

Walk/run through a series of cones.

Walk/run, holding a partner's hand.

Walk/run, in a conga line, holding the shoulders of the child directly in front of him/her.

Walk/run over a series of parallel lines, 12-18" apart, without touching a line.

Walk/run over a series of parallel suspended strings. Begin with a string 1" above the floor and gradually raise the strings until the strings are at the child's ankle level.

Walk the length of the ladder, touching only the rungs.

Walk the length of the ladder, with feet inside the ladder, on the floor, without touching the rungs.

Walk/run with her hands on specific body parts. For example, "Can you walk with your hands on your head?"

Walk/run on tiptoes.

Walk like a "soldier."

Modifying the variable of FORCE, ask the child to:

Walk, holding different weighted grocery bags in each arm.

Walk, while pulling a partner seated on a scooter.

Walk, while pushing a partner seated on a scooter.

Walk with a 3# weight in one hand; no weight in the other.

Walk with a sand-filled teddy bear held in two hands above the head.

Modifying the variable of FLOW, ask the child to:

Walk like Dorothy, the Tin Man, the Lion, the Scarecrow, Toto, and the Wicked Witch of the West, after reading the "Wizard of Oz."

Walk/run forward, turn 180 degrees, walk backward.

Walk/run forward, turn 360 degrees, walk backward.

Walk/run forward. Stop and touch toes. Walk forward.

Ask the child to run, using the following music:

Simon Says Jog Along   Get a Good Start
Chug a Long Choo Choo   Preschool Aerobic Fun
Run, Run, Run in Place Preschool Aerobic Fun

Locomotor Skills: Jump/Hop

Modifying the variable of TIME, ask the child to:

Jump/hop to a drum beat or hand clap.
Jump/hop to music with a 2/2 or 4/4 beat.
Jump/hop following the bouncing of a ball.
Jump/hop in slow motion, to the bouncing of a balloon.

Modifying the variable of SPACE, ask the child to:

Jump/hop over a line on the floor.
Jump/hop over and back, across a line on the floor.
Jump/hop over and back, across a line, side to side.
Jump/hop in an "X" pattern over lines that cross on the floor.

Play "Sizzling Snake." Make a jump rope slither on
the floor and have the children jump to
avoid being bitten.

Jump/hop over a set of two lines, with ever
increasing distance between the lines.
The child will inherently choose the distance
that is challenging, self-testing, but possible.

Jump/hop reaching to touch a suspended balloon.
Jump/hop reaching to touch a suspended balloon,
three times in a row.

<u>Modifying the variable of FORCE, ask the child to:</u>
Play "Kangaroo."
The child assumes an erect body position with
flexion only at the knees and ankles. She
springs to complete extension and then flexes
to land. This is much more fun if the child
wears her backpack on her chest, pretending
it's her pouch. It is even more fun if the child
carries a teddy bear or doll in the pouch.

Play "Jack Be Nimble"

> The child jumps over an object on the floor,
> while you and the children recite the poem,
>
> > Jack be nimble, Jack be quick.
> > Jack jump over the candle stick.
> > Jack jump high, Jack jump low,
> > Jack jump high or burn your toe.

Play "Jumping Bean."

> The children jump while reciting the poem:
>
> > Have you seen my jumping bean?
> > Strangest thing I've ever seen.
> > It jumped off my plate,
> > And on to the floor.
> > Suddenly, it jumped out the door.
> > Jump, jumping bean, jump.

Play "Peter Cottontail."

> The children hop while reciting the poem:
>
> > Here comes Peter Cottontail,
> > Hopping down the bunny trail,
> > Hippity, Hoppity,
> > Spring is on its way.

<u>Modifying the variable of FLOW, ask the child to:</u>
Jump forward 2 times, hop on right foot 2 times,
        jump forward 2 times, hop left foot 2 times.
Play hopscotch.

Jump forward 1, backward 1; jump forward 2,
   backward 2; jump forward 3, backward 3;
   forward 4, backward 4.
Hop forward 1, right 1, left 1, backward 1.
Jump forward 2, backward 1, forward 2. Jump
   backward 3 times; stop; jump backward 3
   times.

Locomotor Skills: Gallop/Slide

Modifying the variable of TIME, ask the child to:
Gallop to the theme of the TV show "Bonanza."
Gallop while a partner claps hands every time the
   child's foot strikes the floor.
Slide to an uneven beat.

Modifying the variable of SPACE, ask the child to:
Gallop on a pattern -- Figure 8, circle, or stop sign.
Slide around every rectangle on the gym floor.
Play "follow the leader," following a classmate who
   gallops and slides about the gymnasium.

Modifying the variable of FORCE, ask the child to:
Gallop, while lifting and springing as high as
   possible.
Slide, while keeping feet as close to the floor as
   possible.
Gallop, while using "baby steps."
Slide on tiptoe; slide on the heels.

Modifying the variable of FLOW, ask the child to:
Gallop forward 3; stop; gallop forward 3.
Slide right 4 times; stop; slide right 4 times.
Move in a square. Gallop forward and backward.
   Slide sidewards.

Locomotor Skill: Wheelchair Roll

Modifying the variable of TIME, ask the child to:
Roll to the beat of a drum, tambourine or hand
        clap.
Roll, varying pace, using songs like "Song about
        slow, song about fast" or "Freeze."
Roll, starting from a stop, accelerating through a
        distance.
Roll, with a partner, pushing every time the
        partner's foot strikes the floor.

Modifying the variable of SPACE, ask the child to:
Roll between two lines.
Roll over the top of lines forming shapes or
        patterns -- circles, squares, triangles, and ovals.
Roll around, between, and through cones,
        classmates, chairs, or desks.
Roll on a variety of surfaces -- grass, carpet, sand,
        cement, linoleum, etc.
Roll up and down inclines.
Roll over door jams, sticks, small stones, etc.
Roll backwards, eventually repeating the above
        activities, but backwards.

Modifying the variable of FORCE, ask the child to:
Use one "max" push to roll as far as possible with
        one push.
Use two "max" pushes to travel as far as possible
        with two pushes.
Roll, pulling a classmate on a scooterboard.
Roll, with a classmate seated on his lap.

31

Modifying the variable of FLOW, ask the child to:
Roll forward 3 strokes; stop; roll backward
        3 strokes.
Roll forward, pivot 180 degrees, roll forward.
Roll backward, pivot 360 degrees, roll backward.
Complete an obstacle course that includes moving
        through cones, over 2 X 2's, moving
        up and down ramps, and doing "wheelies."
Modifying the variable of TIME, ask the child to:
Clap slow; clap fast.
Clap to a cha cha beat.
Bend and touch the floor; stretch to the sky. Start
        slowly, and build up speed.

Non-Locomotor Skills: e.g., Clap, Bend, Twist and Stretch

Modifying the variable of SPACE, ask the child to:
Clap, using little claps; clap, using huge claps.
Clap, up and down; clap, side to side.
Clap, moving the hands in diagonal patterns, to
        make an "X."
Twist, alternately touching either foot.
Stretch in all directions, becoming as "big" as
        possible; then tuck into a tight ball.

Modifying the variable of FORCE, ask the child to:
Clap hard; clap soft.
Bend, going "around the world." Bend front, to the
        side, to the back, to the other side; change
        direction and go back the other way.
Twist trunk to the right hard; twist to the left
        gently.

Modifying the variable of FLOW, ask the child to:
Clap 1 time; stop; clap 2 times; stop; clap 3 times.
Bend forward; stretch; hold. Bend backward;
        stretch, hold.
Clap, twist, stretch, and bend...in sequence.
Stretch to the sky; stretch to touch toes. Repeat.
Clap, twist, stretch, or bend to the shaking of a
        tambourine.

MOTOR PLANNING

Bobble Balloon, Bobble Balloon
Ask the child to begin bobbling [keeping it in the air]
one balloon using any body part. Then, tie two balloons
together and ask the child or children to bobble the
two balloons. Continue to add balloons, tied together
at the knots. Tied together, they float oddly and are
fun for the children to track.

Keep the Scarves in the Air
Ask the child (or a group of children) to keep one scarf
in the air. Then, gradually, add another scarf, so the
child or group of children keep two, then three, then
four scarves in the air at the same time.

Balloons and Scarves and Feathers
Ask several children to, alternately, keep a balloon and
a scarf and a feather up in the air at the same time.
As the children demonstrate their ability to keep the
three items in the air, add extras.

Square Away -- Beachball

Ask two children to each grip two corners of a scarf or towel. Working together, the children use the scarf or towel to fling a beachball in the air. Working together, the children catch and then fling the beachball again. The children can count, together, the number of times they are successful.

Square Away -- Yarn or Koosch Balls

Ask two children to each grip two corners of a scarf or towel. Working together, the children use the scarf or towel to fling the yarn or koosch ball into the air. Working together, the children then add another ball, until they are carefully flinging "lots" of balls and catching them in the scarf.

Circle Around

Ask the children to sit in a circle. To a rhythmic beat in a favorite song, ask the children to begin passing an object about the circle. Start with one object. As the children become more proficient, add more objects. In order for this to be an effective motor planning activity, it is critical that the objects differ widely. Include the following:

> 4" yarn balls
> 12" playground balls
> 8" slightly deflated beach balls
> stuffed animals
> wooden blocks
> lemmi sticks
> 3" koosch balls
> animal bean bags [Sportime has cute ones.]
> nerf footballs

When the children are moving the objects around the circle to the beat, ask them to stop and change direction [from clockwise to counter-clockwise].

34

Catch the Popcorn
Ask the children to keep different colored beachballs "popping" on a parachute. One or two children drop their hold on the parachute. They should try to catch a particular, colored beachball while it is popping.

Alex's Dance
Ask all the children to be seated in a circle. Ask the first child to "show me" a movement, any movement, she likes to do while seated. The teacher helps the children integrate the movement with the child's name.

> For example, "punching the air" with one fist can be paired with the child's name. "Al-ex," "Al-ex," "Al-ex," punching on "Al" and returning to flexion on "ex."

All the children do Alex's movement together.

Then, the next child in the circle shares his movement. The teacher helps the children combine the movement with the child's name.

> For example, "clapping" while paired with the child's name. "Chris-to-pher," "Chris-to-pher," "Chris-to-pher," while clapping on each syllable.

All the children do Christopher's movement, and then, Alex's movement, in sequence. Add a new child's movement after each repetition.

The teacher can help gauge the number of children who should participate in each "circle activity" based on the developmental age and readiness of the children. Eventually, add music to this process to turn it into a dance.

Popcorn

Ask the children to keep different colored beachballs "popping" on a parachute. One or two children drop their hold on the parachute and try to hit a particular, colored beachball back on the parachute.

Scooter Sharing

Ask two children to share one large scooter. [Sportime has wonderful "megascooters" that two children can share.] Ask the children to work together to move about the room in a designated direction or path.

Flowing Streamer

Ask one child to lead the group, and the rest of the children follow the leader's movements. The leader has his back to the group, and does exaggerated movements with his arm/hand holding a streamer. The leader should be creative, yet move the streamer slowly enough so the other children can follow.

Sensational Streamers

Ask one child to lead the group, and the rest of the children follow the leader's movements. The leader has her back to the group, and does exaggerated movements with her leg/foot with a streamer tied to her ankle. The leader should be creative, yet move the streamer slowly enough so the other children can follow.

Choo Choo

Ask a group of children to stand, in a line, facing each other's backs, holding the hips of the child in front. The children, as a group, try to walk together, forward and then backward, without falling. Add more complex locomotor tasks as the children can handle it:

> Jumping
> Hopping
> Sliding
> Galloping

Toss and Catch

Ask a child to toss and catch [to self] a beachball. At first the child should stand. Then, ask the child to do the self "toss and catch" while:

> Kneeling on one knee
> Kneeling on two knees
> Long sitting
> Cross legged sitting
> Lying on her back

Dribble

Ask a child to dribble a large playground ball. At first, the child should stand. Then, ask the child to dribble while:

> Kneeling on one knee
> Kneeling on two knees
> Cross legged sitting
> Lying on his back.

When the child has mastered all these skills, ask the child to keep dribbling while moving from position to position.

Diamond Play
Ask two children to sit in a long sitting "V" position, facing each other with feet touching to make a diamond. Keeping their feet touching they keep the balls in the diamond, and they should keep as many balls [of varying styles, shapes, and textures] moving at the same time.

Partner Bounce
Ask two children to stand 3' apart and bounce an 8" playground ball to each other. When they have been successful, ask the children to take a step backward and bounce the ball to the partner at a distance of 5'. Increasingly, when successful, ask the children to bounce the ball from a distance of 10', 15', and 20'.

Throw-A-Way
Ask a child to stand 3' from a partner, and toss gently to the partner. Then, gradually, have the thrower move backward so she is throwing, with ever-greater effort, from an increasing distance -- 5', 10', 15', 20', 25', 30', etc.

Kick-A-Way
Ask a child to stand 3' from a partner and kick gently to the partner. Then, gradually, have the kicker move backward so he is kicking, with ever-greater force, from an increasing distance -- 5', 10', 15', 20', 25', 30', etc.

Movement Sequences

Ask the child to move in sequences that enhance the child's motor planning skills, for example:

Roll right 3 times; roll left 3 times.

Walk to a set of 4 stairs; walk up; walk down.

Run in and through a series of cones.

Run; crouch and jump on 2 feet; run.

Jump; run; jump.

Vertical jump 3 times; horizontal jump 3 times.

Alternately jump forward, then backward.

Jump 2 times, hop right 2 times, jump 2 times, hop left 2 times.

Hop right 1 time, hop left 1 time, hop right 3 times, hop left 3 times.

Hop, hop, hop, jump.

Gallop 3 cycles. Slide right 3 cycles. Gallop 3 cycles.

Clap "big" 3 times; clap "little" 3 times; clap "big" 3 times.

Jump and clap at the same time, 5 times.

Jump; bend and touch toes; jump.

Jump; jump and turn 180 degrees; jump.

Movement Exploration

Ask the children to move in a variety of ways:

Move on four body parts. Then, move on 3 body parts.

Move another way on 3 body parts.

Move yet another way on 3 body parts.

Move forward on a scooter, lying prone, using all 4 body parts; using 3 body parts; using 2 body parts; then using only 1 body part.

Catch a rolled ball using 4 body parts; using 3 body parts; using 2 body parts; then using only 1 body part.

OBJECT CONTROL SKILLS

Dump and Fill

Fill an empty box or a laundry basket with bean bags, koosch balls, yarn balls, and soft stuffed animals. Dump the contents out on the floor and ask the children to put the "stuff" back in as quickly as possible. First, have them use their hands. Then, have them use their feet. Then, later, challenge them to refill the contents using their elbows, or chin and shoulder, or one foot and one knee. The more novel the task, the better.

Stack and Crash and Re-Stack

Ask the children to stack empty shoe boxes, cereal boxes, soft blocks, etc. as high as possible. Then, ask one child to knock the stack over and ask the children to re-stack the boxes, as quickly as possible. First, have them use their hands. Then, have them stack using their feet, and other combinations of body parts to encourage creativity and significant body-part coordination.

Paper Boxes

Ask the children to stuff paper bags with crumpled newspaper. Stuff lots of crumpled wads of newspaper into the paper bags. When the bags are stuffed, wrap and seal them with masking tape or duct tape. Make a stack of the "boxes" and crash and re-stack.

Feather Catch

The teacher stands on top of a stool or chair and drops a feather for several children to try to catch. Add more feathers as the students become better able to track the feather and catch it.

40

Scarf Blowing

Ask the child to lie down on his back. Put a scarf over the child's mouth and nose and ask the child to blow the scarf up into the air. Then ask the child to "catch" the scarf using a number of different body parts.

> Catch the scarf with your elbow.
> Catch the scarf with your nose.
> Catch the scarf on your ear.

Bag the Leaves

Ask the children to crumple large numbers of newspaper into balls. Stuff them into large, empty plastic bags. Let the children jump on the "leaves" and then re-stuff them when they fly out of the "pile."

Clean Up Your Own Backyard

Erect a "fence" made of folded mats, a sheet hung over an extended rope, etc. Divide the children into two groups. Scatter hundreds of balls, yarn balls, beach balls, stuffed animals [anything that will not hurt a child if hit by one] and ask the children to throw or put the objects on their side...into the other children's backyard.

Snow Ball Fight

Use white yarn balls or clean white socks [rolled into balls] to have a snow ball fight. This is a particularly good activity for the "Winter" theme.

41

Oscar's Garbage Can

Ask children to throw and put yarn balls, beach balls and soft stuffed animals into Oscar's garbage can. Oscar, and any friends in there with him, throw the garbage out as quickly as his classmates throw it in.

Texas Round Up

Blow up hundreds of balloons and put them on a parachute. When the cowboys and cowgirls are ready, let the "little doggies" loose [fling them off the parachute] and ask the children to get them back into the corral [the parachute]. Encourage the children to use their feet to "round out" the cattle. If a child needs to use hands...that's cool.

Race Car Driver

Ask a child to hold onto a hula hoop with both hands and, pretending that is the car's steering wheel, drive all around the room, zooming and curving.

Balloon Tennis
Ask two children to play "tennis" using their hands and a balloon. The net can be any obstacle the children need to hit the balloon over. Then, ask the children to use their elbows, knees, feet, and head to hit the balloon back and forth.

Bean Bag Toss
Put a huge target on the ground so the children can't miss it. Ask the children to toss -- underhand, sidearm and overhand -- beanbags onto the target.
Then, put a huge target on the wall so the children can toss -- underhand, sidearm and overhand -- beanbags at the target.

Kitchen Tools are Friends
Dump lots of bean bags and koosch balls on the floor. Ask the children to use typical kitchen utensils to carry the bean bags and koosch balls to a designated container. Use:

        Tongs
        Pancake turners
        Ice cream scoops

Rebound and Catch

Ask the child to sit, with legs spread in a "V" position, with feet touching a wall. The child keeps a ball rebounding from the wall, using both hands.

Self Bounce and Catch

Ask the child to hold a large playground ball, drop it, and catch it at waist level. Then ask the child to drop and catch the ball at:

> Head level
> Shoulder level
> Knee level
> Ankle level.

Bounce and Catch with Partner

Ask two children to play bounce and catch with an 8" or 12" playground ball from a distance of 5'. Gradually, the children should step backward so they are bouncing and catching from greater distances.

Water Balloons

Outside, ask two children to toss and catch a balloon partially filled with water. With young children don't overinflate the balloon. Ask them to start 2" apart and then gradually move backward, trying to catch the balloon without breaking it.

Wall Kick

Ask a child to start with a ball, kick it to a wall, and then kick the rebound. Start close to the wall and move back, gradually, as the child gains control.

Suspended Ball Kick

Suspend a soccer ball, or any other ball that can be kicked safely. Ask the child to kick the ball, repeatedly, using each foot.

Partner Kick

Ask two children to share a playground ball. The children should start close together and tap the ball back and forth. As they develop control, they can move further and further back.

CROSS-LATERAL   INTEGRATION

Mixed-Up Creeper

Place a rope or taped line on a mat or on a carpeted floor. Ask the child to creep while moving forward. As the child creeps forward, her right hand should be placed on the left side of the rope. As the child creeps forward, her left hand should be placed on the right side of the rope.

17 Pick-Up

Scatter 17 blocks, large marbles, dominoes, or small plastic dinosaurs on the right side of the child's body. Holding the child's head still, ask the child to pick up the objects with the right hand and place them, one at a time, in a can placed on the left side of the child's body. Repeat, having the child move the objects with the left hand.

Note: The size of the objects should be determined by the child's fine-motor coordination skills. In order to focus on cross-lateral integration, the child should move objects she or he can hold and control with ease.

Crossing the River

Ask a child to lie supine on a scooter and pull self hand-over-hand along a heavy rope (tug-of-war type) suspended 18"-24" above the child's body. The child should move head first, pretending that she or he is crossing a river. Preferably, the river is full of crocodiles, or alligators, or anything else that makes the activity fun.

Crossing the River, II

Ask a child to lie prone on a scooter and pull self hand-over-hand along a heavy rope (tug-of-war type) that is stretch out on the floor. The child should move head first, pretending that she or he is crossing a river.

Crazy Cross-Over

Place a straight tape line on the floor. Put red objects on the left side of the line and blue objects on the right side. Ask the child to crawl or creep or knee walk along the line. As she or he moves along, the child should pick up the red objects with the left hand and place them over the line, on the right side of the line. The child should pick up the blue objects with the right hand and transfer them to the left side of the line.

Note: The child should only move one object at a time and should keep shoulders perpendicular to the line of travel.

The child can transfer the objects using kitchen utensils:

> Tongs
> Pancake turner
> Ice cream scooper

Pat-a-Cake
Simply play "pat-a-cake." It is a great activity to develop cross-lateral integration.

Pillow-a-Way
The teacher and the child should sit, kneel, or stand facing each other. They should join hands with arms crossed in front of their bodies. Ask another child to place a pillow on top of the crossed arms. The teacher and the child should try to keep the pillow on the arms while swinging the arms back and forth, up as high as possible.

Sawing Logs
The teacher and the child should each hold the ends of a broom handle. Then, they should pretend they are sawing large logs, "sawing" in large, broad strokes, over and over.

Vibrator Vibes
Put a small vibrator in the child's right hand. Call out body parts and ask the child to "vibrate" that part on the left side of the body -- the left elbow, the left knee, the left thigh, the left ankle, etc. Make sure the child does not turn the shoulders or the head while crossing the midline of the body with the vibrator.

Twist-Over
Place a rope or low balance beam on the floor. Ask the child to walk with a "scissors" gait -- the right foot is placed on the left side of the rope/beam and the left foot is placed on the right side of the rope/beam.

Mirror-Mirror

Ask the child to mirror the teacher's movement. Move specifically so that the child will need to cross the midline of the body, i.e., touch right hand to left shoulder, left hand to right foot, etc.

Walker, Texas Ranger

Ask the child to hang from a horizontal bar. Ask the child to kick his/her left leg up and across the midline of the body to kick a pillow (bank robber, bad guy) held in front of the right side of the child's body.

Repeat, asking the child to kick the right leg up and across the midline to kick a pillow held on the left side of the child's body.

Crazy Kicker

Ask a child to sit, with back against a wall. Roll a ball to the right side of the child's body, and ask the child to kick the ball with the left foot. Repeat, with the other foot. Make sure the child keeps his/her back square against the wall.

Stack a Block

Place an assortment of blocks on the right side of the body. Ask the child to pick up one block at a time and make a stack of blocks on the left side of his/her body. Repeat, asking the child to move blocks from left side of body, with left hand, and place blocks in a stack on the right side of the body.

Crazy Spinner

Ask the child to lie prone on a scooter and spin self by alternately crossing hands. Ask the child to spin clockwise, and then counter-clockwise.

AEROBIC FITNESS

Young children, with and without disabilities, must be given every opportunity to use their bodies, actively, and often throughout the day. It appears that young children require <u>at least</u> 30 minutes per day of vigorous aerobic activity.

Children whose potential to perform activities that stimulate the cardiovascular system in traditional ways -- running, climbing on playground apparatus, and tricycling, for example -- need to have the opportunity to move vigorously in other ways.

Music they choose is a very effective tool for encouraging participation.

Aerobic activities that can be performed while sitting are an important activity for a child using a wheelchair or crutches, for a child with an equilibrium deficit, for a child who has difficulty maintaining an appropriate activity level, or for a child who has difficulty with impulse control.

Any aerobic fitness regiment must begin with a warm-up.

Warm-up Activities
Simultaneous Shoulder Shrugs
Ask the children to shrug both shoulders simultaneously. The cue, "Try to touch your shoulders to your ears, " appears to work well.

Independent Shoulder Shrugs
Ask the children to shrug first the right shoulder, then the left, alternately. Again, the cue, "Try to touch your shoulder to your ear," works well.

Shoulder Circles
Ask the child to roll his/her shoulders forward. Then, have the child roll his/her shoulders backward.

Transition Activities
Huge Hand Claps
Ask the children to clap their hands. At first, the claps should be little. Gradually, the children should begin making the clapping motion bigger and bigger.
The children should vary the claps:

> Horizontal
> Vertical
> Diagonal

Eventually, all muscles of the arms and shoulder girdle should be involved.

Clap Thighs-Clap Hands
Ask the children to take both of their hands and clap on their thighs. Then, they should clap hands together. Repeat the motion, gradually making the motion bigger and bigger.

Aerobic Activities
Simultaneous "Above the Head" Punches
Ask the children to reach both hands toward the sky at the same time, holding hands in a fist. Allow hands to return to the lap to recover. Repeat the motion.

Simultaneous "In Front of Chest" Punches
Ask the children to punch the air in front of their chests by moving arms from flexion to extension, holding hands in a fist. Return hands to the lap to recover. Vary the activity by having the children open and extend their fingers during the "punch."

Simultaneous "To the Sides" Punches
Ask the children to punch the air, moving both arms from flexion to extension at the shoulder level to the sides. Relax by returning hands to lap. Repeat.

Alternating Punches
Perform any of the above punches -- above the head, in front of chest, and to the sides -- but alternate arm action. One arm should be in extension while the other is in flexion.

Hands on Hips Twist

Ask the children to put their hands on their hips and twist their trunks to the right, and then to the left, while sitting in an erect posture.

Trunk Twist, Arms Extended to the Side

Ask the children to hold their arms extended to the side at shoulder level. Alternately, twist trunk to the right and then to the left, while maintaining an erect posture.

X-Cross in Front

Ask the children to hold their arms out to the sides at shoulder level. Keeping the arms straight throughout, draw arms toward and then past the midline of the body. Alternate which arm is "on top."

Cross Over the Head

Ask the children to hold their arms above their heads. Keeping arms straight throughout, move one arm forward in front of body and one arm backward.

Butterfly

Ask the children to hold their fists near their armpits and move their arms, flexed at the elbows, like butterflies, rapidly up and down.

Arm Pumping (Simultaneous)
Ask the children to hold both arms with elbows bent so there is a ninety degree angle at the elbows. Pump the arms forward and backward simultaneously.

Arm Pumping (Alternately)
Ask the children to hold both arms with elbows bent so there is a ninety degree angle at the elbows. Pump the arms, alternately, forward and backwards, as if "running" while sitting.

Both Hands Toe Touches
Ask the children to sit erect. Then ask the children to bend down to touch both toes and then return to a fully erect position.

Alternate Hands Toe Touches
Ask the children to sit erect. Then ask the children to bend to touch right hand to left foot, and then, left hand to right foot.

Arm Circles to the Sides
Ask the children to sit erect. Holding both arms straight out to the sides, the children should start by making small circles and build to making huge arm circles.

Arm Circles Over the Head
Ask the children to sit erect. Holding both arms, straight, above the head, the children should begin by making small circles and build to making huge arm circles.

Trunk Stretch with Beachball
Ask the children to hold a beachball above their heads. Ask the children to sit erect and stretch to the side, right , and then to the side, left.

Jumping Jack Arms
Ask the children to hold their arms at their sides. Then, keeping the arms in line with the children's bodies, move to clap the hands above the head and return the arms to their sides.

Warm-Down Activities
Trunk Circle
Ask the children to sit erect, and slowly circle their trunks, first clockwise and then counter-clockwise.

Head and Neck Circle
Ask the children to sit erect, and slowly circle their heads, first clockwise and then counter-clockwise.

Hand, Wrist and Forearm Wave
Ask the children to hold their hands at head level, with palms facing away from the body. Ask them to move their hands, wrists and forearms like "wiper blades" on a car.

RELAXATION ACTIVITIES

Basic Relaxation Position
The children can practice basic relaxation techniques in a sitting or lying position. If relaxation is to be practiced while sitting, the back should be straight, the head in alignment, and feet should be flat on the floor. Hands and arms should rest comfortably on the desk or the lap.

If lying, it is important that the children have their backs flat on the floor with arms and legs rotated away from the midline position. If a child is unable to lie on the floor with back flat, it may be necessary to put a pillow underneath the child's knees.

Deep Breathing Exercise

Encourage the children to be aware of their own breathing. Simple techniques to encourage this include:

- Ask a child to put her hand on her chest to feel it rise and fall.
- Lay a scarf on the child's face [child lying on back] and ask the child to "breathe out" and make the scarf move.
- If the child is having difficulty sensing this, ask the child to put her hand on the teacher's chest while the teacher exaggerates the inspiration and expiration process.
- Ask a child to put his hand in front of the nose/mouth of a partner to feel the expiration.

Once the children are aware of their respiration rates, ask the children to slow down their breathing. Repeat the process, reminding the children to be aware of the air coming in and the air going out. It will often take as many as five minutes before the children are able to actually slow their respiration rate.

Head and Neck Circle

Ask the children to assume an erect sitting or standing position. Ask the children to slowly rotate their heads in a full circle five times in one direction and five times in the other direction. Some children may prefer to keep their eyes open to prevent dizziness. Repeat, as needed. Combine this with the deep breathing exercise.

Shoulder Rolls
Ask the children to assume an erect sitting or standing position. Ask the children to slowly roll their shoulders, forward in a whole circle and then, slowly, roll their shoulders backward. This is particularly effective when combined with deep breathing exercises.

Imagery Techniques
It is important for the teacher to be sensitive to the fact that what might be relaxing to one child may be frightening for another. For example, one child may find the image of lying on a sun-baked beach near a lake to be very relaxing while another may be desperately frightened of water. Some images that may be effective, without being frightening for young children include:

Sleepy Puppy or Sleepy Kitty
Ask the children to pretend to be a sleepy puppy or kitty, curling up to go to sleep. Ask the children to alternate stretching and yawning and then curling up to go to sleep.

Melting Ice Cream Cone
Ask the children to pretend to be an ice cream cone melting in the hot sun. Combine this with deep breathing exercises.

Progressive Relaxation-Facial Muscles

Ask the children to assume a sitting or back lying position. Ask the children to tighten their face muscles. This can be accomplished by asking the children to "crinkle" the face to look like a "raisin" or a "prune" and, then, to relax. This can also be done effectively by asking the children to make their faces look "mad" and, then, to make their faces "happy."

Repeat the process for several minutes. Begin to ask questions to help the children become more aware of the sensations, "Can you feel the difference when your face is "mad" and "happy?"

Progressive Relaxation - Arm Muscles

Ask the children to tighten the muscles in their arms. The best technique for eliciting this response is to ask the children to "make a fist" and squeeze. Alternate tightening and relaxing for several minutes. Combine with deep breathing.

Progressive Relaxation-Abdominal Muscles

Ask the children to tighten their stomach muscles. This is best accomplished if you ask the children to put a hand on the stomach and press the stomach in. Alternately contract and relax; combine with deep breathing exercises.

Progressive Relaxation-Leg Muscles

Ask the children to tighten the muscles in their thighs. Ask the children to put a hand on a thigh [demonstrate] and then ask them to "make the leg 'hard.'" Then ask the children to relax and let the leg get softer.

Progressive Relaxation-Whole Body

Ask the children to tighten the "whole body." Using cues like, "make your body like a rock," may help the children understand. Then, ask the children to relax and "let your body be like a wet noodle."

My Safest Place

Lead the children though a series of carefully controlled "visions" to help the children picture the place, time or setting that allows them to feel safe and relax. It is important not to create the scene, but rather to allow the children to create their own scenes. This is vital because what is relaxing to one child may be very frightening to another. In fact, some children may not have anywhere where they feel safe.

Use leading statements like,

- "Picture the place where you feel safest."
- "Picture the place where you most like to sleep."
- "What does your favorite spot look like?"
- "Can you imagine being there?"

COOPERATIVE GAMES

Parachute Play - Peek and Wave

Ask the children to sit around a parachute [or a tie-dyed sheet or sheet decorated by the children with Magic Markers] and grasp the edges. One child at a time crawls under the parachute into the center of the circle. Given a signal, the children on the outside of the circle lift the parachute and then drop one hand and wave at the child in the center while shouting the child's name. The child in the center waves back. This activity can be excellent for facilitating language, particularly when working with children who use English as a second language.

Parachute Play - Ripples and Waves

Ask the children to sit around the parachute and grasp it with both hands. Have the children move the parachute edge up and down 4"-6" to cause "ripples." Then, ask the children to move the parachute edge up and down 12"-18" to cause "waves." Let one child "swim" on the parachute, first through the ripples and then through the waves.

Parachute Play - Launch the Rocket

Ask the children to kneel or stand around the parachute and grasp the edges with both hands. Place a huge "earth ball" or "beachball" on the center of the parachute. Ask the children to work together to coordinate efforts to "launch" the rocket to the ceiling.

Parachute Play - The Magic Mountain

Have the children grasp the edges/handles of the parachute. Make sure that the parachute is flat on the ground before you begin. On a given signal, the children should lift the parachute up over their heads and then, together, pull parachute to ground "trapping" the air and, then, holding the edges to seal the air in the mountain. Then, allow children to use a locomotor skill they "own" to move over the top of the mountain

- Roll
- Crawl
- Creep
- Knee walk
- Wheelchair roll.

Parachute Play- Trapped Under the Magic Mountain

Repeat the above activity. But, this time, as the parachute is brought down to the ground, have the children move under the parachute so when they trap the air, all the children are caught under the magic mountain. The children can count together to see how long the mountain stays up in the air.

Parachute Play - Find Your Spot

Have the children sit or stand and hold the parachute. One by one, each child should drop hold of the parachute and use one of the following locomotor patterns to go around the parachute and, then, retake his or her original spot:

- Wheelchair roll
- Walk
- Run
- Jump
- Gallop
- Slide

Parachute Play- Don't Get Trapped

Have the children sit or stand and hold the parachute. One by one, each child should drop hold of the parachute and uses a locomotor pattern to go under the parachute and take a spot on the other side. [Note: In the non-cooperative game, the children holding the parachute try to "trap" the child while under the parachute; in this version, the children try to keep the child underneath from being trapped.]

Parachute Play- Spoke of the Wheel

Ask the children to each grasp the parachute with one hand, each child using the same hand. Then the children, as a group, using the same locomotor pattern, move about the parachute center as if the parachute is a wheel.

Parachute Play - Circle the Ball

Ask the children to grasp the edges or handles of the parachute. Working together, the children must get a large ball rolling around the perimeter of the parachute. [Note: It looks a lot like doing a "wave" at a football or basketball game if the kids can get the ball going.]

Parachute Play - Keep it Popping

The children try to keep hundreds of kernels of popcorn [koosch balls, bean bags, yarn balls, beach balls] popping on the parachute. [Note: In the typical parachute popcorn game, the children try to pop the popcorn off the parachute; in this game, the children have to work together to keep the objects on the parachute.]

Don't Let It Touch the Ground

Using balloons and beachballs have a group of children try to keep the balloons or beachballs up in the air, using any given body part -- hands, head, feet, elbows, or knees. Initially work in small groups; as the students develop cooperative play skills, enlarge the group and increase the number of balloons and beachballs in the air.

Together Now

Ask the children to get into a line and perform the SAME locomotor activity. Children in wheelchairs can be involved by having a partner help, if needed, move the wheelchair. Ask the children to line up, hold each other by the waist and perform one of the following:

• Walk forward/walk backward
• Run forward/run backward
• Jump forward/jump backward
• Slide to the right/slide to the left

Modified Musical Chairs
Set up the play area as if you were going to play a typical game of "musical chairs." But instead of having a child eliminated if the child can't get find a seat, let the children share chairs. Eventually, as more and more chairs are removed, three or more children will be sitting on each other...sharing a chair. At the end of the game, ALL the children will be sharing the final chair.

Hug Tag
Play a game of tag with the following simple modification. A child is "safe" if the child is hugging another child. Eventually, modify the game so the only time a child is "safe" is if she or he is involved in a group hug with 3 or 4 children.

Sardine Can
Ask the children to lie down on their stomachs, tightly squeezed together side-to-side. Have one child lie down at one end of the line of children and roll [wearing no shoes or braces] across the sardines and take her new place at the other end, tightly squeezed next to the child who had been last.

Hot Potato
The children are seated in a circle and can use hands or feet to pass an object -- bean bag, nerf ball, large playground ball -- around the circle as fast as possible to avoid getting "burned."

Sit With Me
One child sits with his/her legs apart in a V position on a chair. The child calls out the name of a child and says, for example, "Ernesto, come sit with me." Ernesto comes and sits down on the child's lap. Then Ernesto invites another child to sit on his lap, and so on. This can also be done sitting on the floor or in the grass.

Water Balloon Pass
The children get in a long line and pass a water-filled balloon from one end of the line to another without breaking the balloon.

Follow the Leader Over the Obstacle Course
One child is the leader. It is the leader's responsibility to choose a movement pattern that everyone in the group can use to follow the leader over the obstacle.

Fill the Water Table
The children get in a line and pass a water -filled plastic bucket down the line from the water source to the water table. The goal is to fill the water table using as few buckets as possible. The group can keep a tally.

Let's Go Fly a Kite
Ask the children to work in twos, threes, or fours to literally "fly a kite."

Beach Ball Pass

Ask the children to sit in a circle or in two lines facing each other. Using a huge beachball, ask the children to pass the ball back and forth and keep it in the air, not letting it out of the circle or over the line. At first, use the hands. Then, use the feet. Later, ask the children to be creative about what body parts they can use to hit/pass the ball -- the knees, elbows, and ankles.

Body Pass

Ask the children to lie down on their backs, close together, like sardines in a can. [The children should alternate so one child's head is next to another's feet, and vice versa]. Ask them to put their arms out straight and to "pass" a friend from one end of the line to another. The child being passed should lie on his or her back, being "straight like a stick."

The teacher will need to help the children get started. Place stronger children next to children lacking strength. The teacher should travel with the child being passed to "spot."

Pinball Marching Marvel

Ask the children to stand in a circle, facing out, with feet wide apart and touching. Then, ask the children to lean over so their "backsides" are facing the center of the circle. Putting hands down, have them use their hands like pinball paddles to keep a large ball moving across and about the circle.

A child in a chair can simply use his or her arms as paddles at the sides of the chair. A child who needs to remain in a lying position can be one of the "bumpers."

Partner Stand Up

Ask two children to sit with backs facing each other. Have them intertwine arms and then push with their feet, simultaneously, to a standing position.

This takes strength and coordination and may need to be practiced [a lot!]. However, the children must work together to accomplish this goal.

The Creature

The game begins as a simple game of tag. One child is designated as "it." When "it" tags a person, s/he joins hands and "creature" gets larger and larger as each child is tagged. The children must hold hands as they encircle and tag each new child. When all children are part of the "creature," the game begins again.

While typically played with children walking or running, this wonderful game can be modified so the children can be crawling , creeping, jumping or hopping creatures. The teacher can tie a bandana or yarn around the thighs of two children creeping or jumping together, etc.

Sitting Volleyball-Forever
Any number of children can play, but there should be the same number of children on each side of the net. Players should be seated on either side of a low net [suspended not higher than 1' above the average extended hand height of the children].   The intent of the game is to keep the beach ball going back and forth over the net as many times as possible.

Just One More
Identify one shape or object. Ask one child to get into an object and invite other children in until no more can fit [reminiscent of stuffing people into telephone booths or Volkswagen Beetles during the 1970's.] For example, use:
- Hula hoops
- Nap mats
- Cloth tunnel
- Refrigerator box

Elastic or Rubber Band Shapes
Ask three or four children to work together to form a given shape with a huge rubber band or large piece of elastic. The children should have the chance to form basic shapes. Then the children can play "Just One More" inside the created shapes.

SUGGESTED   MUSIC   AND   SONGS

Tony Chestnut and Fun Time Action Songs. The Learning Station. 800.789.9990

Easy Does It: Activity Songs for Basic Motor Skill Development.   Freeport, NY: Educational Activities, Inc., Activity Records Inc., 1977.
>Bean Bag
>Circle Your Way
>High Wire Artist

Greg and Steve. *Kidding Around with Greg and Steve.* Los Angeles: Youngheart Records, 1985.
>The Hugging Song
>Believe in Yourself
>Hokey Pokey, Part 1 and 2

Greg and Steve. *We All Live Together, Volume 2.* Los Angeles: Youngheart Records, 1979.
>Popcorn
>The Freeze
>Resting

Vince Junior. *Cows and Other Assorted Fun Songs for Children.* Azracer Records. 413.269.6242

Tom Knight and Elizabeth McMahon. *Peanut Butter and Jelly's Greatest Hits.* Tom Knight Productions, Alcazar Music. 800.541.9904

Mod Marches. Freeport, NY: Educational Activities, Inc., Activity Records Inc., 1970.
>Penny Lane
>It's a Small, Small World
>Yellow Submarine

Hap Palmer. *Creative Movement and Rhythmic Exploration*. Freeport, NY: Educational Activities, Inc., Activity Records Inc., 1971.

> Moving Game, Part 1 and 2
> Colored Ribbons
> Teacher Who Couldn't Talk
> Percussion Instruments

Hap Palmer. *Pretend*. Freeport, NY: Educational Activities, Inc., Activity Records Inc., 1971.

> The Friendly Giant
> The Clown
> Jumping Frog
> Kite Song

Hap Palmer. *Sally the Swinging Snake*. Freeport, NY: Educational Activities, Inc., Activity Records Inc., 1987.

> Sally the Swinging Snake
> On the Count of Five

Hap Palmer. *Seagulls for Rest and Relaxation*. Freeport, NY: Educational Activities, Inc., Activity Records Inc., 1987.

Hap Palmer. *Walter the Waltzing Worm*. Freeport, NY: Educational Activities, Inc., Activity Records Inc., 1982.

> What a Miracle
> Walter the Waltzing Worm
> Flick a Fly
> Song About Slow, Song About Fast
> Swing, Shake, Twist and Stretch
> All the Ways of Jumping Up and Down

Six Little Ducks. Classic Children's Songs. KIMBO, Box 477, Long Branch, NJ, 07740.

Georgiana Stewart. *Bean Bag Activities and Coordination Skills.* KIMBO, Box 477, Long Branch, NJ, 07740.

> Who's Got the Bean Bag?
> Bean Bag Rock
> Pass the Bean Bag
> Bean Bag Parade

Georgiana Stewart. *Preschool Aerobic Fun.* KIMBO, Box 477, Long Branch, NY, 07740.

> Wake-Up, Warm-Up
> Hot Diggity
> Movin' Every Day
> Chug a Long Choo Choo
> Run, Run, Run in Place
> Consider Yourself
> Marching Along Together

Toddlers on Parade: Musical Exercises for Infants and Toddlers. KIMBO, Box 477, Long Branch, NJ 07740.

Jessica Baron Turner and Raney Susan Schiff. *Let's Make Music. Multicultural Songs and Activities.* Hal Leonard Carpenter. 800.637.2852

RECOMMENDED EQUIPMENT

SPORTIME
One Sportime Way
Atlanta, GA 30340
800.283.5700
http://www.sportime.com

SUGGESTED REFERENCES

Cherry, C. *Creative Movement for the Developing Child: A Nursery School Handbook for Non-Musicians.* Belmont, CA: Lake Publishers, 1971.

Doray, M. *J is For Jump! Moving into Language Skills.* Belmont, CA: Lake Publishers, 1982.

Hillert, M. *Let's Take a Break: Exercise Poems for Young Children.* Continental Press, Elizabethtown, PA, 1981.

Huettig, C. and O'Connor, J. *Wellness Programming for Preschoolers with Disabilities.* TEACHING Exceptional Children, 31(3): 12-17, 1999.

Pyfer, J. *Motor Development Evaluation and Programming,* Texas Woman's University, Denton, TX, 1986.

Roth, K., Huettig, C., & Andersson, E. Healthy Activities for Young Children. Dallas: Women, Infants and Children of Dallas, 2000.

Schurr, E. *Movement Experiences for Children: A Humanistic Approach to Elementary School Physical Education.* Englewood Cliffs, NJ: Prentice Hall, 1980.

Sillberg, J. *Games to Play with Toddlers.* Beltseville, MD: Gryphon House, 1993.

Warren, J. *1-2-3-Games: No-Lose Group Games for Young Children.* Everett, WA: Warren Publishing, 1986.

Young, S.B. *Movement is Fun: A Preschool Movement Program.* Torrance, CA: Sensory Integration International Publishers, 1988.